# Comments on the original Theory is Fun books.

As a music teacher, I have all my children and adults start with this little book. The basics of music theory are laid out succinctly and clearly, with accompanying short exercises.

Dr T J Worrall

I'm a music teacher, and can honestly say this series of books is by far the most concise and fun to work with when helping kids. Adults also enjoy them.

C J Gascoine

Very thorough and approachable theory practice book for young students age 7 upwards.

Susan A. Harris

Theory can be a barrier for some young students but this book is set out well, it's easy to read and understand, and has logical progression. Highly recommended.

Steve Riches

I might at last be able to learn my theory and I am an old age pensioner learning to play the piano.

Violet

Very good book that puts things very simply. I was recommended this by my piano teacher even though I am an adult learner as it covers all the technical points very progressively.

Amazon Customer

GW00683382

## Music Theory is Fun Book 1

978-1-987926-09-5
Treble clef, bass clef, notes and letter names. Time names and values. Dotted notes, tied notes and rests. Accidentals, tones and semitones. Key signatures and scales (C, G, D & F major). Degrees of the scale, intervals and tonic triads. Time signatures and bar-lines. Writing music and answering rhythms. Puzzles, quizzes and ten one-page tests. Musical terms dictionary and list of signs.

## Music Theory is Fun Book 2

978-1-987926-10-1

Major key signatures to 3 sharps & flats. Minor keys to 1 sharp & flat. Degrees of the scale and intervals. Tonic triads. Keyboard, tones and semitones. Time signatures. Grouping notes and rests, triplets. Two ledger lines below and above the staves. Writing four-bar rhythms. Puzzles, quizzes and ten one-page tests. Musical terms and signs.

## Music Theory is Fun Book 3

978-1-987926-11-8
Major & minor key signatures 4 sharps or flats. Harmonic and melodic minor scales. Degrees of the scale, intervals, tonic triads. Simple and compound time signatures. Grouping notes & rests. Transposition at the octave. More than two ledger lines. Writing four-bar rhythms, anacrusis. Phrases. Puzzles, quizzes and  ten one-page tests. Musical terms & signs.

## Music Theory is Fun Book 4

978-1-987926-12-5
Key signatures to 5 sharps or flats. Alto clef. Chromatic scale, double sharps & flats. Technical names of notes in the diatonic scale. Simple & compound time, duple, triple, quadruple. Primary triads, tonic, subdominant & dominant. Diatonic intervals up to an octave.  Ornaments. Four-bar rhythms and rhythms to words. Orchestral instruments and their clefs. Puzzles, quizzes and ten one-page tests. Musical terms & signs including French.

## Music Theory is Fun Book 5

978-1-987926-13-2
Key signatures to 7 sharps or flats. Tenor clef and scales. Compound intervals:  major, minor, perfect, diminished & augmented. Irregular time signatures, quintuple & septuple. Tonic, super-tonic, subdominant & dominant chords. Writing at concert pitch. Short & open score. Orchestral instruments. Composing a melody. Perfect, imperfect & plagal cadences. Puzzles, quizzes and ten one-page tests. Musical terms and signs including French and German.

## Music Theory is Fun – A Handy Reference

978-1-987926-10-1
A concise reference to all the rudiments of music covered by the above five Music Theory is Fun books.

## Music Theory is Fun: Books 1 to 5 Omnibus

ISBN 9781987926156

This omnibus edition is the complete set of the newly revised series of five separately published books Music Theory is Fun by Maureen Cox.

Using an attractive layout with clear examples and illustrations together with activities to reinforce learning and understanding, it provides a convenient step-by-step, easy to follow course for anyone learning to sing or to play an instrument, studying the theory of music or revising for examinations. At the end of each book is a collection of puzzles and quizzes and a set of ten one-page tests of questions typically encountered in exams.

## Music Theory is Fun Puzzles, Quizzes & Tests Books 1 to 5 Answers

ISBN 9781987926170

This book gives you the answers to all the puzzles, quizzes and tests at the end of each of the five books in the series Music Theory is Fun.

## Musical Terms Word Search in a Nutshell

ISBN 9780986654992
ISBN 9781987926057

Maureen Cox provides an attractive, easy-to-use book that is an essential addition to her best-selling series MUSIC THEORY IS FUN. Inside you will find the following features: practice in writing the words and meanings; 5 sections graded according to difficulty; 4 word search puzzles in each section; 4 answer grids in each section; alphabetical list of the 40 words of each section; final section at the end of the book to test yourself.

## Musical Terms & Signs in a Nutshell

ISBN 9781987926088

This slender paperback is an attractive, easy-to-use reference book containing more than 400 commonly encountered musical words and signs. The book also contains the treble, bass, tenor & alto clefs, all thirty key signatures and a helpful metronome & tempo guide. It is an ideal companion to **Music Theory Is Fun - A Handy Reference**

## Harmony is Fun in a Nutshell

ISBN 9780986654916

In her latest book on harmony at the keyboard, MAUREEN COX, guides you in a step-by-step, easy way to master the following topics: tonic, dominant and subdominant chords; supertonic, mediant and submediant chords; chords in root position, first and second inversion; dominant 7th chord and its third inversion; chords spread between treble and bass clef; block and broken chords; major and relative minor keys up to 4 sharps or 4 flats; major, harmonic and melodic minor scales; substituting chords II, III & VI for IV, V & I; resolving; perfect, imperfect and plagal cadences; melodic decoration: essential and unessential notes; passing and auxiliary notes; binding notes; modulation; chord progression and fingering; the magic circle of keys. This book is for anyone who wants to have fun learning to harmonise at the keyboard.

# MUSIC THEORY IS FUN
## *BOOK 2*

# Maureen Cox

All enquiries regarding this paperback edition to:

Mimast Inc
email: mimast.inc@gmail.com

Printed by Pardy & Son (Printers) Ltd.,
Parkside, Ringwood, Hampshire, BH24 3SF
Tel: 01425 471433
Fax: 01425 478923

For my grandson Michael

* * * * * *

If you want to play an instrument, sing well or just improve your listening, you need to read music and understand theory.

This book takes you through the theory of music in a simple, straightforward way. There are plenty of fun illustrations and a variety of activities to help you along.

Towards the back of the book there are puzzles, quizzes and ten one-page tests composed of questions you could meet in an exam. At the end of the book there is a dictionary of musical terms and a list of signs for easy reference

With my help you can continue on the road to mastering and enjoying the theory of music. With this book you can discover that Theory is Fun.

Maureen Cox

## Acknowledgements

I am grateful to the many Professional Private Music Teachers and Members of the Incorporated Society of Musicians who used Theory is Fun with their pupils and to Christina Bourne, Brenda Harris, Alison Hogg, Judith Holmes, Ann Leggett and Marion Martin for their helpful suggestions. I am especially grateful to Alison Hounsome for her insightful comments and helpful recommendations in the preparation of this revised edition.

## A word about this revised edition

Using the previous editions of my Theory is Fun books, more than a half million people, young and not so young, mostly in the UK, had fun learning music theory. This edition has been revised and extended to include students in other countries such as America and Canada where, for example, a bar is a measure, a minim is a half note and a tone is a whole step. Common alternatives terms are listed at the back of the book with a dictionary of musical terms and signs.

This book covers the basic rudiments of theory required by the various Boards and Colleges including the Associated Board of the Royal Schools of Music, Trinity College London, the Music Examinations Boards of Australia and New Zealand and the Royal Conservatory of Canada.

Any errors are entirely my responsibility. Should there be any in this edition, I would be most grateful for them to be drawn to my attention so that they may be corrected in a future edition.

Maureen Cox

# CONTENTS

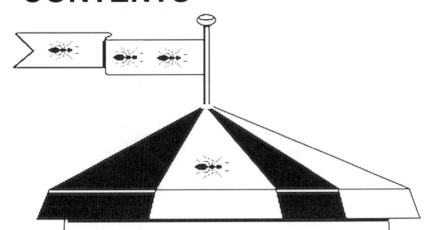

# MAJOR KEY SIGNATURES

In Book 1 you met four key signatures.

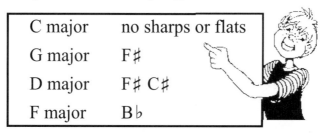

| | |
|---|---|
| C major | no sharps or flats |
| G major | F♯ |
| D major | F♯ C♯ |
| F major | B♭ |

Write letter names of the key signatures for these four keys.

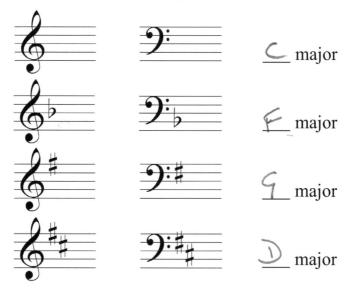

C major

F major

G major

D major

The sharps and flats are always
on the same lines and in the
same spaces for key signatures.

In this Book 2 you meet three new major keys.

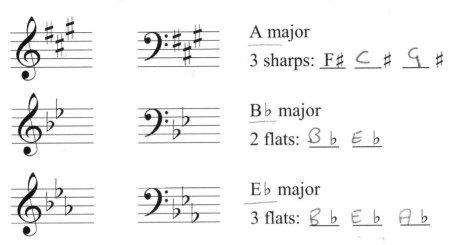

A major
3 sharps: <u>F♯</u>  <u>C</u> ♯  <u>G</u> ♯

B♭ major
2 flats: <u>B</u> ♭  <u>E</u> ♭

E♭ major
3 flats: <u>B</u> ♭  <u>E</u> ♭  <u>A</u> ♭

Practise these major key signatures. This is not a test.

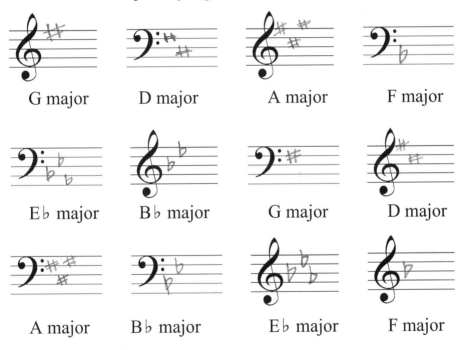

G major     D major     A major     F major

E♭ major    B♭ major    G major     D major

A major     B♭ major    E♭ major    F major

When you are sure of all seven key
signatures, turn the page and test yourself.

## Test yourself

You now know the key signatures for seven major scales up to 3 sharps and 3 flats. You need to remember where the sharps and flats sit on the stave and their order. Clue: for the two sharps in D major think **F**ather **C**hristmas.

D major

F major

A major

B♭ major

E♭ major

G major

Check your answers.

Did you check your answers?

Yes I did. I always do.

8

# Tones and semitones

In Music Theory is Fun Book 1 you learnt about tones /
*whole steps* and semitones / *half steps* by using a keyboard.

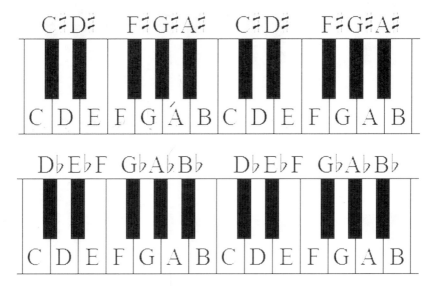

Fill in the missing letter names:

| | | |
|---|---|---|
| F raised one semitone / *half step* | = | F# |
| F raised by one tone / *whole step* | = | G |
| A♭ lowered one semitone / *half step* | = | G |
| G♯ lowered one tone / *whole step* | = | F# |

When you think you can put in all the letter names on a
keyboard, turn the page.

## Test yourself

Write the letter names of the white keys in capital letters on the keyboard below.

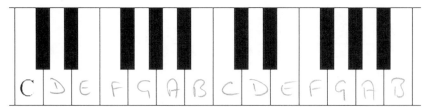

Put the letter names of the white keys in capital letters on the keyboard below and write the names of the sharps above the black keys.

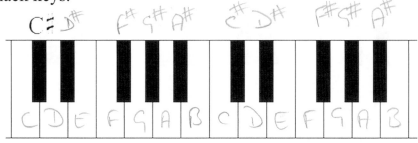

Put the letter names of the white keys in capital letters on the keyboard below and write the names of the flats above the black keys.

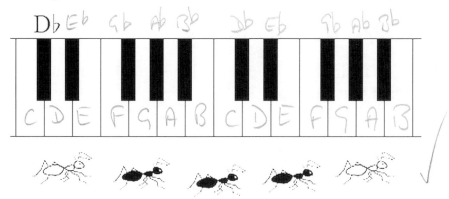

# Semitones / half steps in major scales

In major scales there is a semitone / *half step* between notes 3 and 4 and between notes 7 and 8. Here is one of your new scales – A major – with the semitones / *half steps* marked.

Write with key signature in the treble clef the scale of B♭ major in crotchets / *quarter notes* ascending. Mark the semitones / *half steps* with ⌐‾⌐ .

Write with key signature in the bass clef the scale of B♭ major in crotchets / *quarter notes* descending. Mark the semitones / *half steps* with ⌐‾⌐ .

When you are ready to test yourself on the major scales, turn over the page.

I'm ready for a test.

## Test yourself

Write with key signature in the treble clef the scale of
F major ascending in semibreves / *whole notes*. Mark the
semitones / *half steps* with ⌐‾⌐.

Write with key signature in the bass clef the scale of A major
descending in minims / *half notes*. Mark the semitones / *half
steps*.

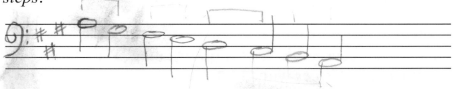

Write without key signature in the bass clef the scale of E♭
major ascending in crotchets / *quarter notes*. Mark the
semitones / *half steps*.

Write with key signature in the treble clef the scale of
G major ascending in minims / *half notes*. Mark the
semitones / *half steps*.

*4 more
to do...*

Write without key signature in the bass clef the scale of D major descending in crotchets / *quarter notes*. Mark the semitones / *half steps*.

Write without key signature in the bass clef the scale of B♭ major ascending in semibreves / *whole notes*. Mark the semitones / *half steps*.

Write without key signature in the treble clef the scale of A major ascending in semibreves / *whole notes*. Mark the semitones / *half steps*.

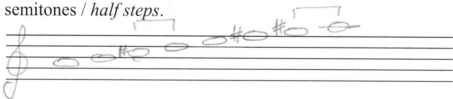

Write without key signature in the treble clef the scale of E♭ major descending in minims / *half notes*. Mark the semitones / *steps*.

13

# MINOR KEY SIGNATURES

## Natural minor scales.

**A minor**: no sharps or flats. A minor is the relative minor of C major. If you count three notes from A you reach C in 3 semitones / *half steps*.

 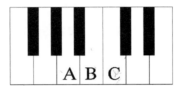

**E minor**: one sharp F♯. E minor is the relative minor of G major. If you count three notes from E you reach G in 3 semitones / *half steps*.

 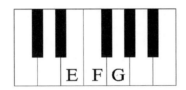 

**D minor**: one flat B♭. D minor is the relative minor of F major. If you count three notes from D you reach F in 3 semitones / *half steps*.

Practise the minor key signatures by writing them in the treble and bass clefs.

E minor                    D Minor

**14**

## Test yourself

How many sharps has

G major?   1 ☑   2 ☐   3 ☐

A major?   1 ☐   2 ☐   3 ☑

D major?   1 ☐   2 ☑   3 ☐

How many flats has

E♭ major?   1 ☐   2 ☐   3 ☑

F major?   1 ☑   2 ☐   3 ☐

B♭ major?   1 ☐   2 ☑   3 ☐

Where are the semitones / *half steps* in major scales?

Between notes 4 & 5 and notes 7 & 8   ☐

3 & 4 and notes 6 & 7   ☐

3 & 4 and notes 7 & 8   ☑

5 & 6 and notes 7 & 8   ☐

On the piano keyboard, if you raise F 3 semitones / *half steps* you go to   G♯ ☑   A ☐   A♯ ☐

On the piano keyboard, if you lower E♭ 3 semitones / *half steps* you go to   B ☐   D♭ ☐   C ☑

Check your answers.   ☐ 12

**15**

Which minor key signature has one sharp?

A ☐    D ☐    E ☑

Which minor key signature has one flat?

F MAJOR - Bb
    Relative

E ☐    A ☐    D ☑

Which minor key signature has no sharps or flats?

E ☐    D ☐    A ☑

What is the relative major of A minor?

C ☑    F ☐    G ☐

What is the relative minor of G major?

A ☐    E ☑    D ☐

What is the relative minor of F major?

A ☐    D ☑    E ☐

Write the key signatures of

A major          E♭ major          E minor

Check your answers.  ☐/9

**16**

# Harmonic minor scales

Harmonic minor scales sound frightening but they are really very easy. All you do is raise the 7th note one semitone / *half step* ascending and descending.

A minor

E minor

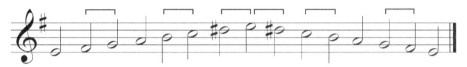

D minor

***Important***
There are semitones / *half steps* (marked ⌐¬) between notes 2 & 3, 5 & 6 and 7 & 8 when ascending and descending.

## Test yourself

Write without key signature in the treble clef the scale of
A harmonic minor ascending in semibreves / *whole notes*.
Mark the semitones / *half steps* with ⌐‾⌐ .

Write with key signature in the bass clef the scale of
E harmonic minor descending in minims / *half notes*. Mark
the semitones / *half steps*.

Write without key signature in the bass clef the scale of
D harmonic minor ascending in crotchets / *quarter notes*.
Mark the semitones / *half steps*.

Time to check your answers.

18

# Melodic minor scales

To write these scales you raise the 6th and 7th notes one semitone / *half step* ascending and lower them a semitone / *half step* when descending.

A minor

E minor

D minor

Semitones / *half steps* are between notes 2 & 3 and 7 & 8 when ascending.

Semitones / *half steps* are between notes 2 & 3 and 5 & 6 when descending.

## Test yourself

Write with key signature in the treble clef the scale of
E melodic minor ascending in minims / *half notes*. Mark the
semitones / *half steps*.

Write without key signature in the bass clef the scale of
A melodic minor descending in crotchets / *quarter notes*.
Mark the semitones / *half steps*.

Write with key signature in the bass clef the scale of
D melodic minor descending in semibreves / *whole notes*.
Mark the semitones / *half steps*.

Time to check your answers.

Write the notes of the following scales ascending on these keyboards. The first scale has been done for you.

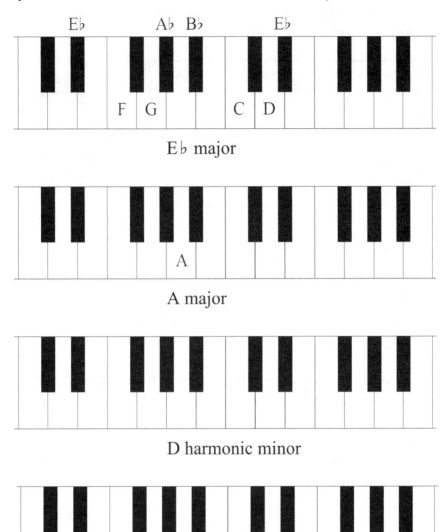

E♭ major

A major

D harmonic minor

E melodic minor

21

## Key signature chart

You have now met the key signatures of seven major scales and three minor scales. Here they are.

| major | key signature | minor |
|---|---|---|
| C | no sharps or flats | A |
| G | F♯ | E |
| D | F♯  C♯ | |
| A | F♯  C♯  G♯ | |
| F | B♭ | D |
| B♭ | B♭  E♭ | |
| E♭ | B♭  E♭  A♭ | |

They are important. You will need to know them if, for example, you are going to take a music theory examination.

In this book, you only need to know the minor key signatures up to and including one sharp and one flat.

If you are given a choice between the harmonic and melodic scales, make sure you say which form of minor scale you are using in your answers.

We should learn
these key signatures.

22

# INTERVALS

In Music Theory is Fun Book 1 you learnt that the first note of a scale is called the keynote or the 1st degree. The second note is the 2nd degree. The third note is the 3rd degree and so on until you reach the 8th degree or octave 8ve.

Write the degree of the scale (1st, 2nd, 3rd, etc.) under each of the notes marked with * in the following passages.

The key is D major.

etc.

The key is E♭ major.

etc.

The number of an interval is the number of degrees in the scale, counting always from the keynote.

For example, in A minor the keynote is A. Therefore, you count each interval from A like this:-

Remember that in minor scales the 6th note and 7th notes might be sharpened. This will not alter the number of the interval.

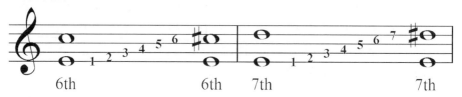

6th           6th   7th             7th

An interval is the difference in pitch between two notes. Let me remind you of melodic and harmonic intervals.

# The melodic interval

This is a melodic interval. The two notes are written one after the other and are played separately.

# The harmonic interval

This interval is called a harmonic interval. The two notes are written one above the other and played at the same time.

## Test yourself

In a melodic interval, always count from the lower note, even if the upper note is written first. Both of these are intervals of a 5th.

Give the number of these melodic intervals (2nd, 3rd, etc.).

The key is E minor.

_____   _____   _____   _____

The key is F major.

_____   _____   _____   _____

Give the number of each harmonic interval. The lower note is the keynote.

_____   _____   _____   _____

_____      _____      _____

Check your answers.

# TONIC TRIADS

The first note of a scale is called the keynote or tonic.

A tonic triad is made up of three notes:-

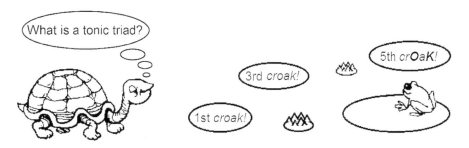

1. The keynote or tonic.

2. The 3rd degree (note) of the scale.

3. The 5th degree (note) of the scale.

Sometimes you will be asked to write a tonic triad with key signature, sometimes without key signature.

So far you have met the tonic triad of D major with its F♯.

| with key signature | without key signature |
|---|---|

With the key signatures that have been added in this book, there are other keys where accidentals occur in the first five notes of the scale.

26

## Test yourself

Write these tonic triads with key signatures.

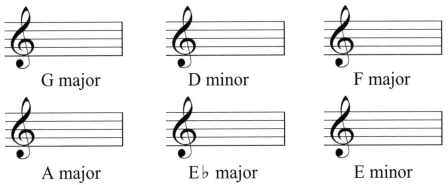

G major      D minor      F major

A major      E♭ major      E minor

Write these tonic triads without key signatures.

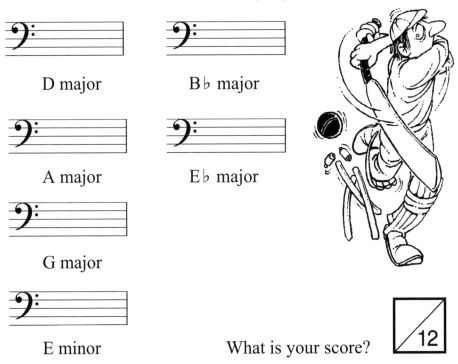

D major      B♭ major

A major      E♭ major

G major

E minor      What is your score? /12

27

# TIME SIGNATURES

In Music Theory is Fun Book 1 you met three time signatures.

The top number tells you how many beats in a bar or measure.

The bottom number tells you what kind of beat.

## Simple duple time

 is the only new simple duple time in this book. It means two minim / *half note* beats in a bar.

## Simple triple time

Here are two new simple triple time signatures.

You can easily work out $\frac{3}{2}$ time – 3 minim / *half note* beats in a bar.

Put one note at each * to make every bar correct:-

Do I need a dotted note?

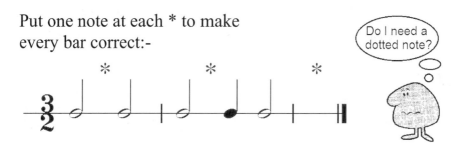

$\frac{3}{8}$ time is 3 beats in a bar – but what kind of beat?

What is the other name for an eighth note?
Yes, a quaver.

$\frac{3}{8}$ time means 3 quaver / *eighth note* beats in a bar.

If the top number is 3,
there are three beats in a bar
and it is simple triple time.

## Simple quadruple time

$\boxed{\frac{4}{2}}$ is the only new simple quadruple time. It means 4 minim / *half note* beats in a bar.

## Test yourself

Add a time signature to each of the following:-

29

## Test yourself

Rewrite these rhythms, as shown in the
first bar, using half the time values.

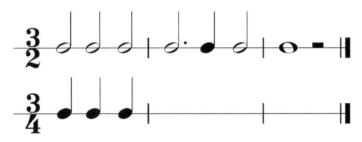

Rewrite these rhythms, as shown in the
first bar, using twice the time values.

Rewrite these rhythms, as shown in the
first bar, using half the time values.

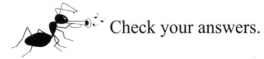 Check your answers.

30

# THE GROUPING OF NOTES

I shall remind you first of the rules for time signatures you met in my Music Theory is Fun Book 1. Then I shall add the rules for the new time signatures in this book.

**2/4 time**

If there are semiquavers / *sixteenth notes*, beam them together into crotchet / *quarter note* beats. Do this too with any group that has a semiquaver / *sixteenth note*.

**3/4 time**

You may beam together a whole bar or measure of quavers / *eighth notes*.

**4/4 time**

You may beam together beats 1 & 2 or beats 3 & 4. Do **not** beam together beats 2 & 3.

DON'T FORGET

What's next?

Let's see. Hurry up

The new time signatures are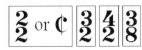

Here are some rules for grouping the notes.

Beam together a group of 4 quavers / *eighth notes* if they could be replaced by a minim / *half note.*

Beam together a group of 4 semiquavers / *sixteenth notes* if they could be replaced by a crotchet / *quarter note.*

If possible, use a semibreve / *whole note* rather than a tied minim / *half note.*

Do not join beats 2 and 3.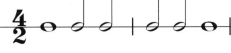

Normally you should not beam together more than 4 semiquavers / *sixteenth notes* but there are exceptions.

You may beam together a group of quavers / *eighth notes* and semiquavers / *sixteenth notes.*

32

Write a whole bar of quavers / *eighth notes* in the times given.

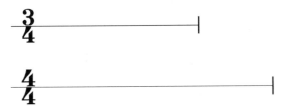

Write a whole bar of semiquavers / *sixteenth notes* in the times given.

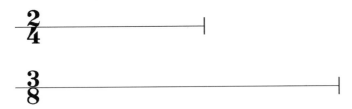

When a group of notes is beamed together all the stems in the

group go either up or down.

If there are two notes beamed together, the note that is further from the middle line has the correct stem. The other note has to follow.

Beam together each group of quavers / *eighth notes*.

Check your answers.

# THE GROUPING OF RESTS

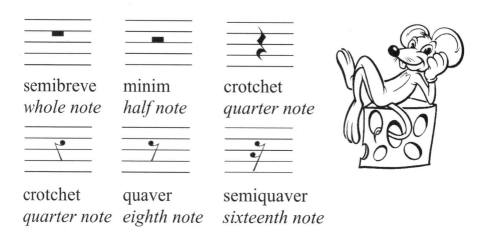

semibreve
*whole note*

minim
*half note*

crotchet
*quarter note*

crotchet
*quarter note*

quaver
*eighth note*

semiquaver
*sixteenth note*

**Whole bar / *measure***

A semibreve rest / *whole note* rest is used for a whole bar with these time signatures. You will not need the $\frac{4}{2}$ whole bar rest until Book 4.

**Part of a bar / *measure***

In quadruple time you can join beats 1 and 2 or 3 and 4.

In triple time rests for beats 2 and 3 must be separate but rests for beats 1 and 2 may be joined.

In duple time each beat needs a separate rest.

Always finish one beat before you start another.

Put the correct rest or rests where you see ★

Check your answers.

# TRIPLETS

A triplet is a group of three notes, or three notes and rests, played in the time of two.

It can look like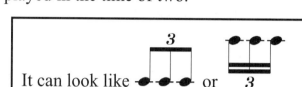

3 quavers / 3 *eighth notes* will be worth 2 quavers / 2 *eighth notes*.

3 semiquavers / 3 *16th notes* will be worth 2 semiquavers / 2 *16th notes*.

A triplet can include rests.

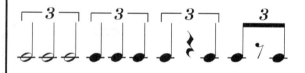

Try these. The first one is done for you:-

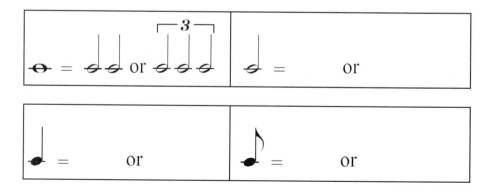

Here are two examples of triplets written for you.

Put a triplet sign [ ⌐3⌐ ] where you think it is needed to make the time signature correct.

Write a triplet of 3 quavers / 3 *eighth notes* or 3 semiquavers / 3 *sixteenth notes* where you see the *

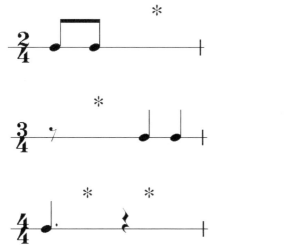

37

# LEDGER LINES

In Music Theory is Fun Book 1 you learnt
the letter names of notes written one ledger
line below the stave in the treble clef and one
ledger line above the stave in the bass clef.

Now you will meet notes on more ledger lines above and
below the stave in both clefs.

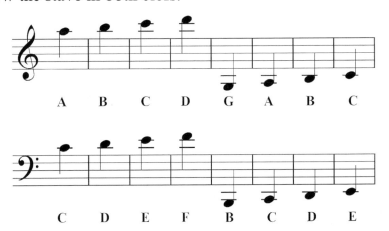

## Friends forever

Sasha was lonely.
She had no-one to play with.

She lived next door to a — — — —

Each day Sasha hoped that a friend would come.

One day, she saw
a dog with a friendly — — — —
at the café.

His name was __ __ __

She __ __ __ __ __ __ her master
to let her out of the house.

Dab was the same __ __ __ as Sasha.

He often came back to the — — — —

Sasha was not lonely any more.

She and Dab stayed friends forever.

## Writing at the same pitch

Here you see a note written in the treble clef. Next to it is the same note written in the bass clef. We say the two notes are at the same pitch.

Write in the treble clef at the same pitch the same note as the one shown in the bass clef.

Write the bass clef notes at the same pitch as the treble clef notes:-

Take care to draw the ledger lines the same width apart as the stave lines.

40

# FOUR-BAR THYTHMS

In Music Theory is Fun Book 1 you were given a two-bar
rhythm with a time signature and asked to write another two
bars. In this book I shall give you the first bar of a rhythm
and ask you to continue writing until you have completed a
four-bar rhythm.

### Handy hints

1. Notice the time signature. Take care to
   follow the rules for grouping notes and
   rests in that time signature.
2. Experiment with different rhythms.
   Tap each one. Which one seems best?
3. Write your rhythms on paper first.
4. End on a strong beat.

Complete each line to make a four-bar rhythm. Try to make
each bar different in some of your answers. If you want the
rhythm to be especially fast (or slow) put Presto (or Lento) at
the beginning.

# PUZZLES

# QUIZZES

# TESTS

# Fun page

Draw a string for each balloon.  I drew the first for you.

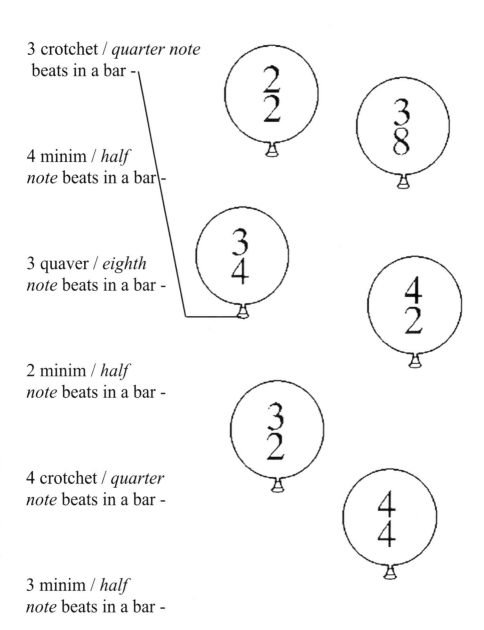

3 crotchet / *quarter note* beats in a bar -

4 minim / *half note* beats in a bar -

3 quaver / *eighth note* beats in a bar -

2 minim / *half note* beats in a bar -

4 crotchet / *quarter note* beats in a bar -

3 minim / *half note* beats in a bar -

43

# Musical Matchword

Can you join the boxes to make ten musical words? I have joined the first one for you.

| | | |
|---|---|---|
| DEG | ENTAL | _____ |
| TRIP | ADS | _____ |
| LED | VALS | _____ |
| INTER | REES | _____ |
| ACCID | TONE | _____ |
| MIN | JOR | _____ |
| SEMI | LETS | _____ |
| MA | ALES | _____ |
| SC | GER | _____ |
| TRI | OR | _____ |

# Musical Anagrams

**techcrot** / *traquer eton* _____

Clue: A note worth 4 semiquavers / *4 sixteenth notes*.

**dregle sinle** _____

Clue: These are above and below the stave.

**charmion** _____

Clue: For this interval play the notes together.

**comidel** _____

Clue: For this interval play the notes separately.

**veremibes** / *weloh tone* _____

Clue: A whole bar's rest hangs from the line.

**vertinal** _____

Clue: Count from the keynote to find its number.

**icont dratis** _____

Clue: These use the 1st, 3rd and 5th notes of a scale.

**plaquedur** _____

Clue: The time with four beats in a bar.

**pliter** _____

Clue: The time with three beats in a bar.

**pudle** _____

Clue: The time with two beats in a bar.

# Crossword

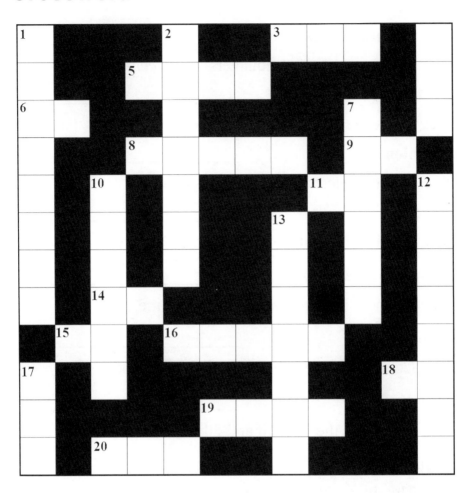

## Clues

### Across

3 hold back, slower at once

5 musical term meaning less

6 short for moderately loud

8 musical term meaning much

46

9 two notes a semitone / *half step* apart

11 an interval of a 5th in C major

14 an interval of a 2nd in G major

15 two notes a tone / *whole step* apart

16 the 1st, 3rd and 5th notes of a scale

18 an interval of a 3rd in F major

19 musical term meaning movement

20 musical term meaning with

## Down

1 the distance between two notes

2 you raise the 6th and 7th notes in this scale

4 musical term meaning more

7 play a group of notes smoothly

10 extra lines above or below the stave

12 short, detached

13 at a walking pace

17 musical term meaning not

47

# Musical terms word search

| | | | | | | | | | |
|---|---|---|---|---|---|---|---|---|---|
| S | A | M | E | N | O | A | C | T | E |
| O | S | A | G | M | S | T | O | S | T |
| S | S | J | I | X | O | Z | E | P | E |
| T | A | S | O | F | I | N | G | H | O |
| E | I | L | C | R | Z | T | E | N | M |
| N | H | O | O | A | A | T | D | Y | A |
| U | J | D | S | T | R | O | P | P | O |
| T | L | O | O | O | G | R | A | V | E |
| O | M | E | F | M | O | T | O | G | T |
| H | M | A | E | S | T | O | S | O | U |

| Meaning | Musical term |
|---|---|
| movement | moto |
| majestically | |
| gracefully | |
| sustained | |
| very slow | |
| too much | |
| without | |
| less | |
| merry | |
| loud | |
| very | |

48

# Quiz 1

Put a tick / *check mark* (✓) in the correct box.

1. **allargando**
☐ at a walking pace
☐ slow, leisurely
☐ broadening out
☐ very quick

2. **larghetto**
☐ faster than largo
☐ slow and stately
☐ very slow
☐ at a walking pace

3. **sustained**
☐ subito
☐ sostenuto
☐ maestoso
☐ ritenuto

4. **held on**
☐ marcato
☐ staccato
☐ subito
☐ tenuto

5. **mosso**
☐ less
☐ more
☐ movement
☐ much

6. **semi-staccato**
☐
☐
☐
☐

Check your answers.  ☐ 6

# Quiz 2

True (**T**) or False (**F**)?

1. The key of C major has no sharps or flats.    **T** ☐   **F** ☐

2. The key of B♭ major has two flats.    **T** ☐   **F** ☐

3. The key of A major has three sharps.    **T** ☐   **F** ☐

4. The key of E minor has three flats.    **T** ☐   **F** ☐

5. The 7th note in a harmonic minor scale is raised one semitone / *one half step* ascending and descending.    **T** ☐   **F** ☐

6. In E♭ major the 6th degree is B♭.    **T** ☐   **F** ☐

7. The two notes in a melodic interval are written one above the other and played at the same time.    **T** ☐   **F** ☐

8. The tonic triad of D minor is D F♯ A.    **T** ☐   **F** ☐

9. The symbol ₵ means 2 minim /*2 half note* beats in the bar.    **T** ☐   **F** ☐

10. A minim rest / *half note rest* is used for a whole bar's rest in $\frac{4}{4}$ time.    **T** ☐   **F** ☐

Check your answers.    ◻10

# Handy hints for tests

This section is for you to practise the different types of questions you could have in a test or an exam.

The questions could be on any topic covered in this book and in Music Theory is Fun Book 1.

Revise each topic in this book thoroughly.

Don't forget to study musical terms and signs – they are **always** included.

Practice
makes perfect !

If you have worked through this book carefully and understood each topic, this will be an easy task for you.

Practice
makes perfect !

Before you begin any test, write out your key signature chart from memory (see page 22). Always refer to the chart when tackling questions that require you to know a key signature.

# Test 1

Put a tick / *check mark* (✓) in the box next to the correct answer.

1. Name this note:

C sharp ☐   A sharp ☐   G natural ☐

2. How many crotchet / *quarter note* beats are in a bar with this time signature?

2 ☐   3 ☐   4 ☐

3. For how many quaver / *eighth note* beats does this rest last?

2 ☐   3 ☐   4 ☐

4. Add the total number of crotchet / *quarter note* beats of silence in these rests.

6 ☐   5 ☐   4 ☐

5. The relative minor of F major is:

D minor ☐   A minor ☐   E minor ☐

6. Name this scale.

G melodic minor ☐
A melodic minor ☐
E harmonic minor ☐

# Test 2

1. Write a triplet of 3 quavers / 3 *eighth notes* or
   3 semiquavers / 3 *sixteenth notes* where you see *.

(a)

(b)

(c)

2. Name the key of this tonic triad.

3. Complete each line to make a 4-bar rhythm.

(a)

(b)

(c)

(d)

# Test 3

1. Write a one-octave E♭ major scale with key signature in semibreves / *whole notes* descending.
   Mark the semitones / *half steps*.

2. Write a one-octave A major scale without key signature in crotchets / *quarter notes* ascending. Put in accidentals where needed and mark the semitones / *half steps*.

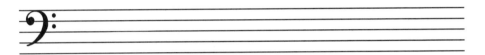

3. Write a one-octave E harmonic minor scale without key signature in minims / *half notes* descending. Put in accidentals where needed and mark the semitones / *half steps*.

4. Write a one-octave D melodic minor scale with key signature in crotchets / *quarter notes* ascending.
   Mark the semitones / *half steps*.

# Test 4

1. Here are four pieces of music. Add a time signature to each of them.

(a)

(b)

(c)

(d)

2. Write a higher note above each given note to make the named harmonic interval.

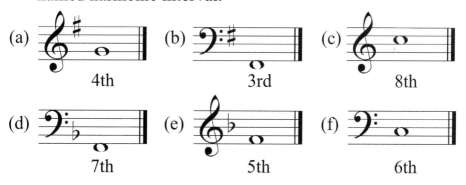

(a)     4th

(b)     3rd

(c)     8th

(d)     7th

(e)     5th

(f)     6th

3. Add the clef and any sharps or flats for this E♭ major scale.

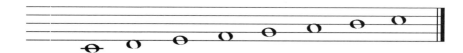

# Test 5

1. Write the letter names for each of the notes marked *.
   Include the sharp or flat.

2. Write the notes in the correct order of the time values
   beginning with the longest and ending with the shortest.

3. Name the keys of these tonic triads.

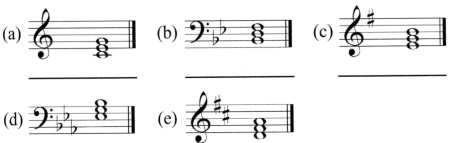

4. Write this passage of music in notes and rests of twice the
   value.

# Test 6

Look at this passage of music then answer the questions.

1. Name the key of this piece.

_____

2. What type of beat is shown in the time signature?

_____

3. How many beats are there in each bar / *measure*? _____

4. What is the meaning of Presto? _____

5. How should you play the two notes in bar 2?

       slowly ☐      smoothly ☐     quickly ☐

6. How many bars have staccato notes?

       6 ☐        5 ☐        4 ☐

7. How many accented notes are there in this piece?

       6 ☐        4 ☐        3 ☐

8. What does *ff* mean? _____

# Test 7

Look at this melody then answer the questions below.

1. Copy the music from bar 5 to the end just as it is written.

2. Name the first four notes in bar 6.

   (a) _____ (b) _____ (c) _____ (d) _____

3. Which two bars have the same rhythms? _____

4. What is the meaning of Allegro? _____

5. Write the letter name of the highest note. _____

6. How should the first two notes be played?_____
7. What does ⌢ mean over the note in bar 4?

   _____

8. Which bar has the note with the strongest accent? _____

9. Name the degree of the scale (e.g. 1st, 2nd) of the first
   note in bar 3. _____

# Test 8

1. This passage of music has no time signature. Work out what it should be and write it in the correct place.

2. Copy out bars 1-4 in the treble clef without a key signature. Remember to write an accidental if needed and to put in the time signature. Write neatly and accurately.

3. Name the major key of the melody. _____

4. Name the minor key with the same key signature. _____

5. Name the notes in bar 7. _____

6. Name the interval (number only) between notes 2 and 3 of bar 2. _____

7. Which bar has the same rhythm as bar 3? _____

8. Circle the note worth 3 crotchets / 3 *quarter notes* in the passage.

9. Circle two notes next to each other which make an octave interval.

# Test 9

Look at this melody and answer the questions below.

1. Find a triplet in the passage and copy it here.

2. Find in the passage two notes next to each other and a semitone / *a half step* apart. Copy them here.

3. Raise each note in bar 1 a semitone / *a half step* and write them here.

4. Lower each note in bar 5 a semitone / *a half step* and write them here.

5. Copy out bar 4 in the bass clef and put in the key signature.

6. Give the meaning of the following:

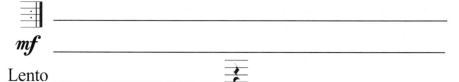

# Test 10

1. This passage of music has no time signature. Work out what it should be and write it in the correct place.

2. Write the notes in bar 4 one octave lower in the bass clef. Put in the key signature.

3. How many staccato notes are there? _____

4. Name the intervals in bar 11 between

    (a) notes 1 and 2 _____

    (b) notes 2 and 3 _____

5. Give the meaning of

*sfz* _____

*mp* _____

< _____

Andante _____

> _____

*f* _____

# MUSICAL TERMS AND SIGNS

# Musical terms

**A** - at, to, by, for, in the style of

**A tempo** - resume the normal speed

**Accelerando** - becoming gradually faster

**Adagio** - slow, leisurely

**Alla** - in the style of

**Alla marcia** - in the style of a march

**Alla polacca** - in the style of a Polonaise

**Allargando** - broadening out

**Allegretto** - slightly slower than allegro

**Allegro** - lively, reasonably fast

**Allegro assai** - very quick

**Andante** - at a walking pace

**Andantino** - a little slower or a little faster than andante

**Assai** - very

**Attacca** - go on immediately

**Cantabile** - in a singing style

**Cantando** - in a singing style

**Col** - with

**Con** - with

**Con brio** - with vigour

**Con moto** - with movement

**Crescendo [cresc.]** - gradually louder

**Da capo [D.C.]** - from the beginning

**Dal segno [D.S.]** - repeat from the sign 𝄋

**Decrescendo [decresc.]** - gradually softer

**Diminuendo [dim.]** - gradually softer

**Dolce** - sweetly

**Espressivo [Espress., Espr.]** - with expression, feeling

**Fine** - the end

**Forte [*f*]** - loud

**Fortepiano [*fp*]** - loud, then immediately soft

**Fortissimo [*ff*]** - very loud

**Forzando [*fz*]** - with a strong accent

**Giocoso** - merry

**Grave** - very slow

**Grazioso** - gracefully

**Larghetto** - faster than largo

**Largo** - slow & stately, broad

**Legato** - smoothly

**Leggiero** - lightly

**Lento** - slowly

**Ma** - but

**Ma non troppo** - but not too much

**Maestoso** - majestically

**Marcato** - strong accent

**Meno** - less

**Meno mosso** - less movement

**Mezzo forte [*mf*]** - moderately loud

**Mezzo piano [*mp*]** - moderately soft

**Moderato** - at a moderate pace

**Molto** - much

**Mosso** - movement

**Moto** - movement

**Movimento** - movement

**Non** - not

**Non troppo** - not too much

**Pesante** - heavily

**Piano [*p*]** - soft

**Pianissimo [*pp*]** - very soft

**Piu** - more

**Pizzicato [pizz.]** - plucked

**Poco a poco** - little by little

**Presto** - very quick

**Prestissimo** - as fast as possible

**Rallentando [rall.]** - becoming gradually slower

**Ritardando [ritard. rit.]** - gradually slower

**Ritenuto [riten. rit.]** - hold back, slower at once

**Scherzando** - playfully

**Scherzo** - a joke

**Senza** - without

**Sforzando [*sf, sfz*]** - with a sudden accent

**Simile [Sim.]** - in the same way

**Sostenuto** - sustained

**Staccato** - short, detached

**Staccatissimo** - very detached

**Subito** - suddenly

**Tanto** - so much

**Tempo** - speed, time

**Tenuto** - held on

**Tranquillo** - quietly
**Troppo** - too much
**Vivace, Vivo** - lively, quick
**Vivacissimo** - very lively

## Common Alternative Terms

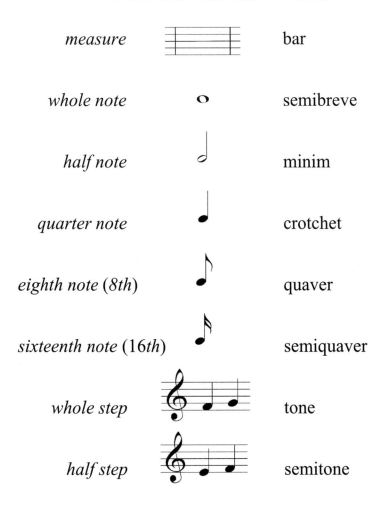

| | | |
|---|---|---|
| *measure* | | bar |
| *whole note* | | semibreve |
| *half note* | | minim |
| *quarter note* | | crotchet |
| *eighth note (8th)* | | quaver |
| *sixteenth note (16th)* | | semiquaver |
| *whole step* | | tone |
| *half step* | | semitone |

# Musical signs and symbols

- tenuto: held on and given full value

- accent the note

- marcato: strong accent

- fermata: pause on the note

- semi-staccato

- staccato: short, detached

- staccatissimo: super-staccato

- tie or bind same notes together

- becoming louder

- becoming softer

- becoming louder then softer

- start repeat and end repeat

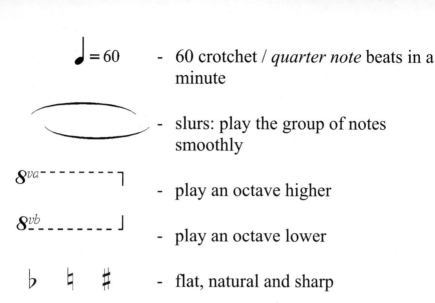

♩ = 60    - 60 crotchet / *quarter note* beats in a minute

- slurs: play the group of notes smoothly

$8^{va}$ - - - - - - - - ⌐    - play an octave higher

$8^{vb}$ - - - - - - - ⌐    - play an octave lower

♭   ♮   ♯    - flat, natural and sharp

treble clef   bass clef

♭s   Battle Ends And Down Goes Charlie Fast

♯s   Fast Charlie Goes Down And Ends Battle